MW00881776

Kill The Poets

Kill The Poets

Sir Tinnley Reel

Writer's Showcase
New York Lincoln Shanghai

Kill The Poets

All Rights Reserved © 2002 by Sir Tinnley Reel

No part of this book may be reproduced or transmitted in any form or by any means, graphic, electronic, or mechanical, including photocopying, recording, taping, or by any information storage retrieval system, without the permission in writing from the publisher.

Writer's Showcase
an imprint of iUniverse, Inc.

For information address:
iUniverse
2021 Pine Lake Road, Suite 100
Lincoln, NE 68512
www.iuniverse.com

Any resemblance to actual people and events is purely coincidental.
This is a work of fiction.
Cover Art By: Adam Rose
Book Design by: Freddy Arroyo

ISBN: 0-595-24512-9

Printed in the United States of America

THE SUSTENANCE

A VERY SPECIAL THANKS TOO:
Benjamin Franklin Pierce
Mary Ellen Pierce
Ben
Mary Anne
Billy
Bobby
Kate
Susan
Joan
Margaret
Tricia
John
Tim
&
Jenny

ALSO

Tracy McCormick
Adam Rose
Freddy Arroyo

CHAPTER 1
PELVIS CHESTON

Sir Tinnley Reel

KILL THE POETS

Kill the poets

My friend, my love

Kill the poets like God above

Hang them on your walls

Tack them to the board

Keep them in the stalls

So you're never bored

Kill the poets

Make them all dead

Kill the poets

By keeping them in the head

FEAR ON A BOOKSTORE SHELF

This world…

Enclosed in an envelope of fear,

Fear to control,

Fear to speak,

Fear to see,

Fear to hear,

Fear of something above,

Fear to have something to be afraid of!

The fear to love,

The fear to accept,

The fear that there is

Nothing left!

The K.K.K.,

The I.R.A,

The next day,

Another way,

Sir Tinnley Reel

Who's to say what we'll

Be afraid of today?

A cigarette smoke,

An artichoke,

Another reason to kill

The old folk?

Another war,

A liquor store,

Second parent dead

On the living room floor?

This world…

What's next?

The fear of ourselves?

Just put it with everything else,

On a bookstore shelf.

MOSAIC

Did you know we are
Controlled by father time
The limits are there
And we must break them
Like a heart

Come with me
In miraculous flight
We'll fall and fall and fall
As life's stifled witness
Stands silent

Come with me
To the largest lake
Dance with me
On the ancient and wise sand
It has seen us come and go
Give birth and die
It knows all
But lies dormant

The sea takes all
That is dirty
And swallows it
Like a last meal into the abyss

Come run with me
And ghosts of time
Past present and future
All is mine

Sir Tinnley Reel

Watch the teary rain
Fall from the sky
The Earth is crying
As it dies

We have been raped
Tortured and beaten
By those who taught us fear
In a Morning Prayer

Let's run now
To a new land
Food friends
And family on a stand
The wine is fresh
And so are our lives

No more crying no more pain
No more of the Earth's teary rain

We scream at the faces
In the mirrors
The faces that fear
Rejections ugly head
Where are my friends
When I need them

We need great leaders
That don't lead
No more following
For you and me
Just listen to this
Troubled decree

Kill The Poets

Oh, my friends,
Fearful self-conscious infection
Has claimed thee

There is a Fire God
Behind this gentle façade

FOR OOEY, GOOEY LOVE PRESS HERE

Late one night, or early morning,
Images of her were gravely growing,
Beating my brain with the beauty she bestowed.
As the thoughts I was thinking,
Like sired ships, were slowly sinking,
In this ocean she controls-
As she does me, like no one knows.
With that beauty she bestows.

She was a Goddess on her shell,
Sailing over ocean swells,
Hammering hearts like hallowed bells
And guiding cello bows.
She caught me like a crook,
As with a trick I took,
A long and loving look-
A look at the beauty she bestowed!
A sight worth stealing, of such, I've never known-
The sight of that beauty she bestowed.

And in this venting, this long lamenting,
There was inventing
Of situations we never showed.
Giving my mind remedies, wrapped around melodic melodies,
Manifesting man made memories
That in reality never flowed.
Dreamed up memories, that in reality never flowed,
Dreams that only I would know.

Fate was flirting; her tide was turning,
There was no telling which way we would go!
There was love and alluring, in her sheets a serpent stirring

Kill The Poets

In the moon lit glow!
The secrets moonlight, that night did show!
I, on top of beauty bestowed!

This is my sight on every single night,
In this, too tight, dream land I have sewn.
The fascination of her face,
Grabbing away all the grace,
Taking away every trace of knowledge I have known.
Slipping from sanity with any knowledge I have known.

This I wish on no other man,
This position in which I stand,
This melting into madness is all I know!
Creating surreal scenes, memories made in dreams!
Hallucinating a history that was never so-
Sewing a seed that will never grow
To reap the beauty she bestowed!

Fading fast I fall asleep, sleeping soundly, begin to dream
Of my beauty the ocean only knows.
Dreaming how to hold her, as I once told her
In a letter long ago.
In a letter I never showed
To my beauty long ago.

I wrote it with perfection, the perfect punctuation
Of the even undulations of the waves
On which she flowed.
Written with a pen,
Fashioned from the stem,
From the realist of the red, red ruby little rose.
Written with the wanton truth of the beauty she bestows.
Yet, this she'll never know.

F

   E

      L

         L

Cigarettes burn away with every breath we take
The gentle haze of booze and dope defiles every room

The thirst is not quenchable
Drink—Clink—Sink
(The void is near)

Eye lids like automatic garage door openers
With the motor stuck on close
Arms and hands and head like lead
Falling—crawling—stalling
(Nap time on cement and blue carpet)
Cool tile would be much better-

Awake-
Arm dead, head half alive
Eyes won't open
Skin crawls and dies-

You touched the other side of the stars last night
Then fell back down.

NOW

My future is the flame

That is burning my past

My present is the spark

That lit the path

And I'm standing

Somewhere in between

Inhaling the smoke

And breathing a dream

Some things do change

But so does everything else

That is why you don't notice

The difference within yourself

Burning the present days of my life

Creating them between never ending nights

Leaving the ashes

Behind, to blow in the wind

Sir Tinnley Reel

And taking another step forward

To once again begin

Mr. Race Man

It's a beautiful morning in Birmingham
A lovely Sunday all across the land
Little girls smiling and laughing
And stomping their feet
On their way to church
Down on Sixteenth Street

Thunder rolls on a clear day
Now there's nothing else to say
Four beautiful babies
All taken away

Oh, Mr. Race Man
When will you stop running?
How do you see yourself
In the mirror?
Oh, Mr. Race Man
The end is surely coming
Hopefully by then
Your cloudy thoughts will clear!

How will you repay them?
All their loved ones and their families?
Oh, Mr. Race Man
What will you do for them?

ABOVE UNDERSTANDING

It's impossible to be someone
In this world full of everyone
Especially when I'm the one
Who wants to be with you

And when all is said and done
There's a different girl under every sun
Burning bright until the next night comes
And another day to think of you

And you know I've been thinking
While I've been drinking
And you know I remember when…

And if I'm truly sinking
Because my boat is leaking
Well, this is the SOS I would send…

There is no one in this world
Who has been so unfurled
By the simple touch
Of such a simple girl

And every night I'm dreaming
And realizing the meanings
Behind every word and every girl
-And every other thing in this world-

There's a secret I've been saving
And it has become an engraving
On my mind, all the time
-I think of my lost little girl-

Every night, I'm in the same moonlight
That same sight that I've seen before
We danced and we sang, I tickled your brain
But something changed
And now we are no more!

Memories are not like dreams
The first exist the latter
Are not what they seem
But I will merge the two
Between me and you
And make my memories and my dreams
Become reality with you

Sir Tinnley Reel

ALWAYS ANOTHER DAY

"The day is so bright and night is so dark,
The dusk, so quiet, dawn, so stark!"

"Every life revolves like this,
Revolves this way.
Every person's life
Is equal to a day!"

At dawn you're born
Alone and cold
Knowing what you know
And learning what you're told

Then comes morning
When you run and play
Observing other children
And listening to what they say

You have your whole future ahead of you
Unknown to the day
Hiding in the darkness
Of where your shadow lays

You meet more and more people
And learn from them too
The whole time trying to find
A face to fit you

"And before you know it…suddenly it's noon!"

No shadow to be found…
"Your true self without a doubt!"

It's time to choose…
"Win or loose-!"
The beaten path
Or untried ground

"So many lives are lost
At the twelve o'one bell sound!"

There's no way around it
Once your choice is clear
And you step into adulthood
With the utmost in fear
Hanging by your fingernails
And the last thread of your best shirt
You dive into real life
Hoping it won't hurt

You struggle and you struggle
To hold onto values and truth
While those around you
Tromp on your lessons from youth

"They lie and they cheat
And they kick their feet
To get to the top of this pile of slop
Where money is God
And the Pentecostal is greed!"

But you're steadfast and strong
With hope in your eyes
You know you can win these battles
In the war of all lies

And the whole time you're fighting
These forces in sight
You're also looking inward
To find what's missing in your life

"You look to your future
Your present and your past
As your shadow grows longer
On the afternoon grass!"

You fight and you search, you search and you fight
Until you see dusk has grown near
Then in your sight, in this cooler light
You see what you've been searching for is suddenly so clear

Silence falls over the battlefield
Of your life and your time
You realize, what you've been searching
Was hidden by the silent sunshine

"It's not in your shadow
Ahead or behind
It's inside your self
Where you finally find…"

…Your own sense of self
Your own frame of mind
As dusk settles in
And your Inner Light begins to shine

Laughing so lovely
You see the world for what it is
Beauty and perfection
Patience and bliss

Then close your eyes as night's subtle blanket
Slowly closes in…

"Sleep old souls, sleep and dream
Tomorrow's another life
And another chance
To be free!"

PAINT ME...

Paint me as the beach
Being beaten by the raging sea!
Holding desolate homes
To drift wood and forgotten stones!

Paint me as the desert
Vast nothingness and hallucinated treasures!
The last stand of sun bleached bones
From a time no one knows!

Paint me as the sunshine
Burning on through time!
Lighting the way
And warming all the children at play!

Paint me as the rain
Coming to clean what man has stained!
Falling such a long way
Only to disappear and return another day!

You may paint me as whatever
You feel the best reflection may be.
All of these traits are in each of us
Some feel them, others only see.
So you may paint me as any of these!
Or as anything!
Because you will always be you
And I will simply be me!

DREM IN A TIME

She is a beauty that sleeps
With the sun beams
And walks with your dreams

The rivers in her eyes
Flow to an ocean deep inside-
Crystal clear blue
Found only by a few
And untouched by time

Her voice tiptoes
To your ears
She speaks so timid
Yet, you always seem to hear-
Every word, every syllable, every sound-
Because when she is there
Nothing else is around

Skin like a breeze
Wrapped tightly in the sheets
She's with you at night
And always in your dreams

Her lips press softly to yours
The mouths open up
As every emotion pours-

You can barely contain it all
And you still need more

Sleeping there silent
She breathes so quiet

Sir Tinnley Reel

You secretly wish
When the sun comes up
She will still be there
Because there is nothing like her
In this world
There's nothing like
Your dream time girl!

SUN SHINE CITY

That one…
Hiding in her designer clothes
Acting like no one knows
That every time she's still
It's just to strike a pose!

She grows…
Only from the outside in
Thinking would never fit in
The super tight shinny pants
That wrap around her skin!

So thin…
She can hide behind a signpost!
I know it's an old joke
But why does the thought of food
Always make her choke?

And so…
What is wrong with girls today?
When asked, they will always say
They do it because men want them
To look this way.

I say…
I don't want you to be sad all the time
It's your smile that makes you fine!
So just do what you want to
The rest will fall in line.

That one…
Don't hide in your designer clothes

Sir Tinnley Reel

Open your mind; show me what you know
If you laugh and make me smile
Your beauty will surely glow!

Is there some way of showing,
Showing that it's not only what's on the outside.
Is there some way of glowing,
Glowing because you're knowing, you're a beautiful sunflower inside!

IN SIGHT

Look in the holes, what could it be?
Something new for your eyes to see!

I picked the lock-
I turned the knob-
No one told me I should stop
And what did I find
In there this time?

Bats in my belfry!
Kooks in my closet!

I wrapped the past
And the future paper on the present can't stop it!

And their little red rat eyes stare-
Grasping and grabbing at my memories hair!
Swing mean, fleeing toward the light
In sight

And in the night I remember so clear
When those rats turned and reared
And jeered my memory so I could hear
Them scream and sneer, nasty at night
In sight

Deep within me, that door is locked
And electric shocked with every "tic"
Of the electric clock-
To keep the bats in the belfry tied tight
Insanity comes with insight!

Sir Tinnley Reel

-WHEN I SLEEP-

On tomorrow or the next
What will come of me?
What hurdles must I leap?
What ties, break free?

When that day is done
With my efforts complete
Will that night bring to me
My last and final sleep?

While I slumber in my bed
And of another life I dream-
Will the shadows silent scream
Take me away from my being?

Lift me up above myself
So I may look down on me
To answer, what my final question be,
"Do you like what you see?"

Then on that moment of truth
The catharsis will set me free
To fly so high above meadows and trees
Reflecting on all I've seen

That night will arrive
For every one, not only me
Are you prepared to tackle your final deed?
And answer the question, " Do you like what you see?"

-confusion & contradiction-

Does the ground invite the leaves to fall?
Or does the tree kick them out, one and all?
Do things happen because they're wanted or because they're willed?
Who's the hero, the murderer or the killed?

My phone rings every time I don't want it to!
And when I'm waiting, the calls don't come through!
I watch the sun rise and fall every day!
And every time another day goes away!

Do you know why you don't have a shadow at noon?
Because that's when your shadow doesn't need you!
It's like when your lighter refuses to be lit-
At that very moment when you most need it!

Do the seasons change only when the previous one is done?
Or does the latter over take the other one?
Does the moon really steal the suns shallow light?
Or does the sun just want to be known at night?

Your eyes shine when I see them in mine!
They become dull and desolate when we're separated in space and time!
And at the very moment when I believe I see the most
Is when I wake up and realize it was a ghost!

Will there come a time when I reap what I sew?
Or have I sewn the stitches too tight for anything to grow?
Will you come to see me one day by surprise?
Or do I have to accept that it may never happen in this life?

Sir Tinnley Reel

No and yes, the answer is a guess!
More or less, to state is to suggest!
I used to think I knew what I know
But that all changes when the confusion and contradictions begin to grow!

COGNIZANT

Under a tapestry lit by electric light
Saturated in the shine of subtle moon light
Sensual secrets slip out in this scene
The thoughts that I think no longer
Limited to dreams

Wonderful words whispered but to no surprise
Don't have the definitions able to describe
The magic madness all this means
The thoughts that I think no longer
Limited to dreams

Elated in the excitement of her eyes
Loving languid limbs where she lies
Searching without success for some seams
The thoughts that I think no longer
Limited to dreams

Quite quietly her quintessence glowed
Illuminating in an instant the passion we showed
With sweet slumber we drift to sleep
The thoughts that I think once again in
Limitless dreams

RATIOS OF REAL?

Whoa!
        Who goes there?
Who treads light upon
            Hard wood floors?
What light is in a sleeping
        Mans eyes?
Who burns the candle at both
Ears in the mind?
                    How is it, the madness
Is so kind?-
              Slow and seductive
The victim knows not even of it's existence.
                        Sleep-
Sleep and see
        All the colors of your lovers
            And your foes-
"What did you do last night?"
"I stood on a street corner in Oslo
And whistled Dixie to seven foot blondes!"

Whoa!
        Who is there?!
Screaming through this silent
             Air!
        Rest no more Mr. Lazybones!
Discipline in sleep
          Makes a tired man.
What is this new
         Insanity that rises
            Swift?
When eyelids lift-

Out the window,
On the floor,
        In the mirror,
    Through the door.

                        This is genocide!!

All dreams must now die?
                The strangest things-
These real-alities,
                These fate-alities,
        Where do they melt away?
Four walls, a ceiling

                    And bells

                    Happiness in blue!

Sun-sun-sun?
        Where did that come from?
                "The east."
The pretty girl said-

                "But the west

                        Is the best!"

I prefer in between!

                        Two eyes—too much

For that couple—
            Who lies beside
        The seeming dead

                        For eight hours?!

Whoa!
        Sounds push the air,
                    Candles extinguish,
Questions are inconsequential-
            Answers, a wish!
Who is that?
            The ghost of tomorrow's
        Dead son-

                Last Tuesday!

Sir Tinnley Reel

Smell the sex—

Sweat!
Warmth!
Energy!
Who is she?!

Don't go to the bathroom
                    No more matches!
Whoa!
                Relax, relax, relax,
Every direction is another way
        And
    Every different way
                            Is another religion,
I don't want to argue anymore!
                            Inside we all hide
Behind the same
        Individual eyes-
                    So close them
And just think, dream, not think-
                    <u>DREAM!</u>

Average Man

You gravitate towards the best
And you push the rest away
Anything average or even less
Will just get in the way!

There's a secret you've been hiding
In your mind you've made it stay
It's the truth that you've been lying
You're not as good as you say!

Just another average man
With nothing special to offer the world
You like French vanilla ice cream
And five foot five blonde haired girls!

But you want to be so much more
So you surround yourself with smiles
That are as false as their façade
And your respectable response to denial!

You believe that they can make you
All you ever wanted to be
But they're just like you
Just average little bumble bees!

We're all just average men
From kings to bums on the street
It's the simple knowledge of this
That will lift you up to see…

The glory that is innate
It's in your fate to be

Sir Tinnley Reel

One of the greatest of the great
Average men to ever be!

WHAT'S MISSING?

In the suffering moonlight-
All that borrowed sunlight-
That will light my future tomorrow,
I see such a distance-
Space and its resistance-
To the mending of a lonely man's sorrow.

Always looking for some-thing,
Never stopping the search!
But I never see this "thing"
From my low and humble perch.

What is it that is missing?
What do I chase every day?
With this obsession am I just pissing
All my real chances away?

Laying in my bed-
Walking through my head-
I don't know if I'll ever find you,
My missing piece-
That won't even tease
My lost mind with a clue.

Sir Tinnley Reel

RUE BRITANIA!

SOMETIMES I JUST WANT YOU HERE
SOMETIMES YOU SHOULD GO AWAY
SOMETIMES I WANT TO HOLD YOU, DEAR
BUT UNFORTUNATLEY THAT'S NOT TODAY

I HELD YOU LIKE A PIECE OF GRASS
SO I WOULDN'T FALL OFF THIS EARTH
I LOOKED AT YOU LIKE A WORK OF ART
BECAUSE I DIDN'T KNOW WHAT YOU WHERE WORTH

NOW, I JUST STARE AT WALLS
AND SQUEEZE MY CANS
'CAUSE GRAVITY'S DOING A FINE JOB
AND I HAVEN'T ENOUGH MONEY IN MY HAND

WALK ON BY MY OLD BEST FRIEND
WALK ON BY NO NEED TO PRETEND
WALK ON BY MY OLD BEST FRIEND
WALK ON BY AND ENSURE OUR END

I THOUGHT OF YOU AS SOMETHING SPECIAL
WELL, I THOUGHT OF YOU AS SOMETHING
YOU TURNED OUT TO BE EVERYTHING
NOT MUCH TO A WORLD OF NOTHING

YOU SMILED WHEN I FELL
YOU LAUGHED WHEN I CRIED
YOU ASKED ME TO TELL ALL
AND SO I LIED!

RUE BRITANIA!!

MOVIN' ON DOWN

I wasn't born to be a saint
But I wasn't conceived in sin
I've got a mother—and a father who ain't
And a whole lot of other kin!

Well, I've had friends and I've had lovers
In fact I've had three
They've been gone oh, so long
And now there's just me!

Now I'm sitting around on a stranger's ground
And that stranger is me
Sitting around without a sound
And no light to see!

Have I lost everything
To latitude and a dream?
Or have I found my very being
In this serene scene?

Sometimes I feel nothing is truth
And nothing will ever be!
But the fact is, I'm not through
Until I am who is me!

SNAFU to SERENDIPITY

Running lights like frightened children
Bouncing to the music and reflecting off mirrored balls
Floods of screams keep on building
Dousing all democracy and electing echoed calls…

…Of colors and flavors
That can't be described
Reality and its powers
Are forced to subside!

The chant of the drums!
Smoke rings around your thumbs!
You scream to the storm as it comes and runs-
Right through you!

Electric light ecstasy!
Seeing through sight mastery?
The true snafu!

Words that are not recognized
Attack you at every turn of your head
Demons will be exorcised
When enemies learn what you've said!

Standing still in a memorizing motion
Trying to negotiate a crazy notion
That in the midst of this madness
Lurks a hint of the spirit of Cadmus
Where is Thebes?

Where are your five thieves?

Dance, darling, dance!
The night is a mere glance in retrospect!
Standing in that stance
Won't improve your chance or what you've spent!

A kiss, a simple, dimple kiss
Caress the cheek to stop the leak in the holy eyes!
Sacred bliss, a simple, sacred bliss
Seamstress of the weak, stitch me an impossible feat-
Where souls collide!

A MEANS TO AN END

Why do I live in fear
When my future seems so clear
When I can't see
What I'm missing?

Riding on this slow ass train
Window's wet from the rain
Where could I be?
Will you listen?

I've got to keep a clear head
My future's foggy up ahead
But I can see
My future glisten!

I'm going to see my friends
They're a means to the end
And it's free!
They're always giving!

Is there a means,
Some means to an end
Within my friends?

Sitting in the lounge car
Foggy sight isn't very far
So I can see!
So I can see again

I wish I was someplace
I wish I had a pretty face

So I could tease!
So I can see again

Is there a means,
Some means to an end
Within my friends?

-COVET-

Every piece of you so excellently chosen
And placed together
Like every petal of a rose
Like every leaf of a tree
Who am I to look unto thee?

Night is like an instant in your eyes
Day, but a dream-
Who am I to distinguish between the skies
When light never leaves your being?

Your face made to have the Gods shudder
Your voice, the sirens stutter
Your hands to hold the muses
Your mind, whatever your heart chooses!

The beauty of a woman in her perfection
That abounds-
The sight of whom makes it impossible
For men not to covet her ground!

Epiphany

Once I saw an image
That seemed right to me
A slightly curved lineage
Holding the idea to be free
Teaching the world the words
That are masked in mystery
And giving the boys and girls
The secrets of life they need!

Some may say it's crazy
Others, just plain dumb
Because following our instincts
Is no longer a rule of thumb

And so I sit and sleep and dream
Of what life could be
If I only listened more closely
To what's inside of me
All these answers coming through
So crisp and clearly
Almost drowned out by the words
The world screams at me

Some may say it's lazy
Others will never know
But I'm not running through life like a lemming
And missing the entire show!

Sir Tinnley Reel

MOTHER, I CAN NOT BE STILL

Amongst this time that spans me
From my birth until I die
I will not stop my ranting
Of something missing in my life

My Mother, more than once, has asked me
Why do I run from town to town
Looking for some lost mystery
That may never be found?

Because my Mother, it's missing
And I can not live until it's found
Its secret is as resisting
As six feet of freshly patted ground

I know it is out there Mother
And I will find it soon, I will!
When that day comes I will mutter
Mother, now I may be still!

LITTLE MISS MILLER

Little Miss Miller, floating on my thoughts
Like a leaf in a river
Or on a breeze it may have caught.
I see your eyes and they're glowing
Like the gold man has sought!
And your hair of flaxen, flowing
On the wind your wings had brought

I recall her by a tree
So lazily laying in the blades
Of hyacinth with me
And frosted forest sage.
In the shade of whispers
I carefully came to kiss her
And stole her heart away.

But something went a rye in the time
We spent, I think,
She never said goodbye, but shortly,
I would seldom see
Little Miss Miller, with her eyes of glowing gold.
Maybe I shouldn't have kissed her
With these lips, so long alone.

Now, she's just a dream, in my mind I do create
Every little scene with every twist of fate.
And in my nights of sleeping
I hear her white wings singing
Into only memories that I have today

DREAMY DAYS

Dream on days-

Why do you play
Where only misfortune lays?

-You've got your
Minds eye on the clouds
To spy on the sky
As the other two
Watch time fly by—

Wake up sleepy head
Get out of bed
There's plenty of time

When you're dead!

-Your dreams are
All you reach for
When you fall
You hit the gas in your mind
But the world, it stalls!

Dream on days-

Why do you say
There is no other way?

-Open your tired eyes
To see the truth
In the sky
Is it much too far
And much too high?

THE NEVER ENDING PART

And I see your eyes locked in on mine
Giving me that look that I can't define
Those colored worlds, so deep in dreams
My little girl, do you know what this means?

I have you and you have me!
Everyone knows the eyes say everything!
So I turn my head to avoid the trap
To avoid the tap—of my mind!
I wish I was blind—but I see you here
Looking at me-
And I know what this means!

Cupid came down; Prometheus lit his arrow
Now there's no turning back
Not today or tomorrow!

The feeling was sparked by the friction of our hearts
When you look at me I fall apart!
And so it starts—THE NEVER ENDING PART!

Obsession

I dream with my eyes open almost every day
I dream of the images that bring the right words to say
Everything I need you to know before you go away
But I fear, with this lack of sleep, I may move too late

You always hold me like the night holds the stars
So when the sun goes down, hold me again in your arms
I shine through you like the muse that bears your name
With out the night the stars would never be the same

There's a trick to this I just can't find the way
Around the smoke and mirrors of the words that I say
Should I stop and just shut-up, let you choose as you may
Or fight for the right to hold onto my one beautiful thing

Close your eyes and see the stars that shine in your brain
That is me doing my best to enter your dreams
So sleep my love, sleep and tell me what you see
If it's the stars and me then you'll know you're the night that I need

THE NEW BIG BOOM

I've got a nephew who is not yet nine
He tells the tallest tales, baby, all the time
He shakes and shooks and shish-cumbas!
Then he laments a longer line...

"The new big boom is in my room!"
His arms spread out as he flew,
"It's got a snake that will eat your eyes!"
He said, as he soared the skies.

He's a knight, no; he's a fireman
He's dark-vador, life savor in his hand
Maybe one day he'll play in a stadium
Or fly a star ship to fight the Aliems!

For Ben (May 31st 1997) 6:oopm Saturday

YOU CAN CALL ME AZURE...

Do you hear the voices? Do you hear them too?
Can you tell me if it's the walls or the door they're screaming through?
In the darkness of this small, wet room
I'm not alone at night. I have my voices to tell me it's alright.
Sometimes, when I feel brave, I look through that crack in the wall,
I see all the people but they don't know at all!
Sometimes I sleep, I sleep real long!
Because the medicine gives my eyelids muscles that are real strong.
Then there are the days I try not to make a sound—Shhhh!
'Cause when the needles come, everything turns around!
There's a nice old lady that comes in here once or twice a week,
I always ask her what her name is but she never answers me.
All she ever does is call me patient number nine,
Gives me my medicine and tells me I'm fine.
I wish I knew my name so I could know something new.
Maybe it's Sylvester or little boy blue!
Oh well, I don't know, but you can call me Azure if you want to!
Because everybody knows that's short for blue!
I'll see you tomorrow, don't worry I'll be fine.
Days here come and go as swiftly as the nights!
Anyway, things could be worse,
I mean, what kind of life would I lead
If when I closed my eyes I couldn't see
Sweet, crazy dreams!

-THANKYOU-

There ain't no point
In making a joint
'Cause it never bends anyway!

And there ain't no coin
That can buy you a join
'Cause it never spends anyway!

And so we live
Together to get
A life we'll never live
Just to see if we can give…

ENOUGH!

There ain't no reason
To rejoice in a season
If it fades anyway!

And there ain't no pleasing
Another person
If they don't give you the time of day…

AND STUFF!

-PICTURE PERFECT STORY-

you said you had questions
About what to do
You had questions about me and you
So if these answers aren't enough to satisfy
I have more answers hidden behind my lies!

My eyes in your eyes
Dreams do come true
I spy in your mind
The eyes you see too!

And so you disappeared for weeks on end
And you reappeared as a mere friend
Some things will change,
Time takes care of that-
But some things will stay the same
Like the feelings that I have!

My eyes in your eyes
You fade with time
I try but you hide
Time changed your mind!

You said you needed to leave and real soon
You said you're leaving, so I did too
You said you're going away, I said goodbye
You said you'd be back someday-
I wondered why!

-SOME SOMETHING-

The strangest days are when I find myself drinking the cheapest wine-
Some may say I loose my mind but I always try and never find
The secrets that are locked behind…

Moon, you are so bright tonight
Floating in the shattered sun light
If I look back behind my eyes
It is the same as the night time sky

Dreams in a book I write
Never meant to see the light of day
Because they fail inside a strangers mind
One that's hoping to find…

Memories I save and hold that fade so fast as I grow old
Soon that day will come when I know all I've seen
And all I've shown, is done.

The Drinks That Make You Smile Can Also Defile-

He thinks he has the cure
He drowns in it everyday
He tries to blur his sight
So that he's blind to his dismay

(He wants to see the light return)

His knees felt weak
As he staggered through his mind
The thoughts he loved so much
He couldn't seem to find

(And he'd try so hard)

He falls deeper out of sight
Deeper in the sea
Trying to fight the waves
The nectar seemed to feed

(And the strangling thoughts against his beating heart)

The drinks that make you think
Can also make you sink

The thoughts he lost
He paid the price and still doesn't know the cost

(All those thoughts he lost!)

PSYCHONAUT

You can't fight desire because when you choose
To douse that fire, that's desire too
And when you die they light a pyre
Because desire doesn't die with you!

The scent of a woman, an aphrodisiac, unreal!
It seems to summon a new kind of feel!
And when I smell it, I start humming
Because I'll be coming in secrets, unsealed!

Don't hide your secrets because when you do
You may regret having lost them too!
You're so frightened of their effect
But the affect matters too!

These things are word play,
Just another way to get through-
This play is word things,
Just another day with you…

On my mind!

Sir Tinnley Reel

BLOW BY BELIEF

If you can sleep
                        Than just feel free
Because you see
                        It might mean
            It's meant to be-
A sleepless night
                        Is time to think
To think and dream

                                    -About one another-
So if you think
                        It's meant to be
Because you sleep
                        You sleep and dream

                                    -Right next to me-
A kiss good night
                        So you see
I too believe

                                    -We're here forever-

THE GREAT GUINNESS TOAST

If Guinness were a man
He'd be six foot two, handsome and tan!
If Guinness were a girl
She'd surely be the most luscious in the world!

Unfortunately,
Guinness is not a dream date
Sent to you by some fantastic
Act of fate-

But if you drink it down on our cue
It could make the person across from you
Look like Elle McPhearson
Or even Tom Cruise!

Now hold your pints up high and tall
Open your throats
And let it fall
A happy Guinness toast to one and all!

Sir Tinnley Reel

-MY SHIP-

It must have been shifting seas that fateful night
I waited for what seemed like forever to hold it in my sight!
But rumor has it; the sea has swallowed it with delight.

Now I have no cruise
To take away my blues.
To take me to where
I'm supposed to be going to!

My ship sank and nobody told me!
My ship sank in the deep dark sea.
It must've been
Just before it was to come in
Because I was sure it was in reach
Just off the beach.

Now which way do I take?
A car can't take me across the sea
To that secret place where people store their dreams!
I need my boat to stay afloat
In this ever changing scene.
My ship sank and nobody told me!

I waited patiently for my time to come
Everyone else was sailing away
Until finally I was the only one,
Standing there staring at the horizon
My hand was shading my eyes from the sun.

Not even a silhouette or puff of smoke
To delight me.
I stood there for days looking at my watch

Kill The Poets

Wondering where my boat could be?
My ship sank and nobody told me!

CHANCE TO PRE-DESTINY

When I sleep, I do indeed dream!
But are my dreams, in reality,
Merely un-experienced memories?

A fortune tellers mind has the ability to leave behind
The present time that exists in everyone else's mind.
So if this is true, is all we do
Merely lived in a pre-destined point of view?

Coincidences and simple little happenings,
Mistaken identity and pleasant little trappings,
De-ja-vu's in an unknown place,
Recognition in a stranger's face!

Planned in pre-destiny or lost in simple chance?
What will be will be or planned circumstance?

In a distant day I stood in your eyes
But I could not see what you had planned inside,
No matter how hard I tried!

So could it be that our dreams
Are merely reflections of up coming memories?

Puzzle (JUST LIKE A...)

When you left today, I couldn't hear you anymore
You're just like a dream that leaves me so sore
I write like a madman in such a sane world
I'm just like a puzzle missing a piece!
Are you that piece?
Under the chair
Just out of reach
Where I can't see!

However long it takes doesn't matter to me
I want a complete picture; I want that missing piece!
I want you to find me when I get lost
I'm just like a puzzle, an incomplete puzzle
Are you that piece?
Left in the box
Will you come find me?
Right now I'm lost!

(She's hiding out again, she's behind the couch I think!)

She's a piece of my puzzle, complete the picture
I'm just like a puzzle with a missing piece
Are you that piece?
Under the chair
Just out of reach!
Come and see what could be!

VOICES

I Have so much on my mind
All the time
It weighs me down
And makes me rhyme

It pushes my pen
Onto this paper
Beats it and bruises it
To be read later

I don't wish to need this
I don't write to read shit-
But everything comes
From my guts—(A hint!)

Violence for peace
Reaction just for release
There is a free bird that I want to seize!

Insanity amongst the insane
Sanity is so plain
Leave me where I'm sleeping
I stand tallest where I lay

I'm fucked up at my best
So very serious while I jest
There's nothing like being alone
Especially when with guests!

SPOT ME AN EGO

The-Attainer-To-That-Which-Everything-Is
Is one who will understand and grab this
Or merely pass it by with a kiss
Because they know what freedom is!

When I walk down the street
It is more of "me" that I meet!
I love you because you are me
And there's nothing else to do! Do you agree?

Everything is nothing in the form of something!
The senses and the mind make these things!
Spot me an ego when one man sings
And I'll show you a sleeper without dreams!

We, the great Gods of all's nothing!
Sitting on Earth's terrace with the night!
We live the non-living, no birth, no dying in sight!
Existence is laughing and crying, that's right!

Everything is its opposite for the same
Reason everything is the same!
Don't worry if I've confused you
Because I'm here and we share a name!

-MAN GOD-

VISIT

Mysticeated moonlight, meaningful and bright,
Whose window will you woo tonight?
Shinning sheen, so skillful in sight,
O'might, o'might it be mine so bright!

Traveling distances through time and space
To light, so lightly, a languid place!
Touch it two times to light a face
With a finger for thought and not disgrace!

If I coax you to come and glow
Will you surrender to day real slow?
Time must tic away, I know,
But the longer you're here the less you go!

YOU ARE MY NIPPLE

You are, to me,
Just an ornament on a tree.
Like a jewel on a ring
Or bubbles in the sea!

All form no function!
An anorexic luncheon,
Like a pacifist punching
Or a free man clutching!

You are beautiful,
You are great!
On my arm,
You accelerate my fate!

But that is all you are!
Something to look at, like the light from a star!
A little spice to a bland suit!
An imagined sound from a long time mute!

Like nipples on a man,
Or chrome on a '57 Chevy,
All you have to do is stand there
And look real pretty!

You are my nipple!

SONGS GONE AMISS

Happy days where have you gone
In the past is not where you belong
Come dance with me again
And teach me a happy song!

Like the one of love and joy
Between a beautiful girl and a beautiful boy
No worries and no stress
He smiles at her in her new dress!

The sun always shines
And the sky never minds
And occasional kiss
From the occasional passer-by!

Happy days when will you return
To teach me to love and learn
How to smile and laugh and play
Instead of want, need and yearn!

No money and the rents due
No love and night will be here soon
No life to share with you
No more singing the happy tunes!

The breeze blows through
Rain makes all like new
And tomorrow is another day
Full of things to do!

Happy days where have you gone
In the past is not where you belong
Come dance with me again
And teach me a happy song!

ANTIQUITY

Antiquity is a part of me
From my head to my feet
All I am and all I see
Antiquity...
Gods in the sky and Gods in the sea
Gods underground and Gods in the trees
But the Gods only see
What you want to believe
Antiquity...
Antiquity is inside of me
From Alexander to Hercules
The ancient wars of Babylon
To Helen's face in my dreams
Antiquity...
A time to remember
A time to enjoy
Antiquity-
I will always be your boy

SKYLARK SINATA

Stacy went to southern France
Like the place you see on bottles
Steven caught a fleeting glance
And decided he would follow

Someone left a picture book
Sitting by the ocean
But, alas at closer look
The pictures were in motion

You never know what you might find
Behind those crazy eyes
Subtle secrets in the mind
That surface with surprise

People will do the strangest things
If given half a chance
Like judge a book by its cover
Or follow you to France

I have seen the little things
Others never know
Silent whispers in the breeze
The wind so beautifully blows

I still see you on that night
When we were right as rain
Did we see beyond our sight
All those crazy things?

CIRCULATION OF PEOPLE

Messed up hair with china eyed stare
Can't walk too far 'cause your legs don't care

Poor little girl, lost in a world
That she didn't even know existed

Moved here from trees and weeds
Doesn't know what it means to just have streets

Poor little girl, lost in a world
But still persisted

Spent another day in the alley she called the valley
She likes to dilly-daily, people call her Sally

Poor little girl, lost in a world
But now she's insistent

Found an escape from the mid-nights gate
A different state with a needle and some faith

Poor little world, just found a girl
Eyes shut and distant

Opened one eye, flying in the sky
Where the cherubs fly, forced to say goodbye

Poor little world, just lost another girl
It's time to change the system

ARE WE?

When the sea fills with grief
And the clouds rain its relief-

When the walls of light
Fall to the velvet blanket of night
And everyone stands silent
In the shaded sight
Of the next days birth,
Somewhere on the other side of the Earth-

Who do you call?
What name do you scream?
Who catches your fall
In these ruby red dreams?

The shadows of mountains
And the piercing staffs of light
Constantly find their seasons to fight.
As man stands insignificant
In the brilliance of there very rights!

Tiny and small, unknown
Too short to be tall
Too tall to be small
In this infinite arcade
Are we anything at all?

SEASON

I wake up to make up with my mind
I'm sorry my darling, for this every time
Every night it's a fight and I get beat
Run to the sun and get burned by the heat
Everyday, I pay, to sit in this seat

She's a world of a girl but not in my system
She screams when she's mean because I don't listen
I don't care for the stare that she's givin'
But when it's done she's the one that I'll be missin'

Another saved me from the other out in the street
I said I was dead and she thought it was neat
Now, alone in her room I feel my needs
I hate myself for wanting to cheat
But the honey of this bunny seems so sweet

I can't find my mind this time to give it a reason
To draw a line this time that fits in the pleasing
Is it cold? I don't know,
Depends on the season.

SOMA FOR THE SOUL

When the days are dark
And the nights are long
When there's nothing to do
And no where to go
All I need is some…

…Soma for the soul!

There's only one place I turn
In times like these
I turn to someone like you
When I want laughter to flow
All I need is some…

…Soma for the soul!

A savior to my spirit
And master of my memory
I know I shouldn't fear it
But don't you ever leave me
All I need is some…

…Soma for the soul!

DAEDAL

Some people say
That today is just another yesterday
And time is just another second away
Distance is space
And that's just a step to another place

But distance can only separate
It cannot divide
In order to do that
You must, first multiply

And if you walk too far
Like a star out of reach
Or you get lost
Like a drop of water in the sea
I will find you
Like every wave finds a beach
Like the light every stargazer sees

"Away" is just a word
That we all have heard
From time to time
As we walk through life
On our search for what we find

Sometimes our choices
Aren't always right
We miss the voices next to us at night
But everything is going to be all right

And even though you are
Out of my sight

Kill The Poets

I hope you are experiencing
All you want in life

It's a daedal situation, I know
But some times you have to open
The intricate
To let the simplicity show

Sir Tinnley Reel

BORED BIG BOY

(To The Tune Of "Now I Know My A B C's")
A
BE
SEEDY
EFFIGY
HEY
HI
JAGGY
ELEMENTARY
CUE ARREST
GEEZ, LOUISE!
DOUBLE VIEW
SEX
WHY?
ANTSY?

Now I know my apogee
Next time catch my perigee!

With The Blink of an Eye

Our minds are a mass

A procession of thoughts

Like lemmings stepping up to the edge

Each hoping to be caught

All these thoughts; like individual personalities

We think up every day

With the blink of an eye

We send them to a shallow grave

What if that one thought

That one, that just fell,

Was the special one

With some truth to tell?

Lost now, forever, is the chance

It will grow

As we sit and ponder the idea

That we'll never know!

Sir Tinnley Reel

SHHH!

SING ME SOFTLY TO SERENITY
SING ME SLOWLY TO MY SLEEP
SING ME SWEETHEART, SING ME SLOW
SING ME SOMEPLACE SECRETS SHOW

SOMETHING SPECIAL, A SERENADE
SOMEPLACE WHERE A SECRETS SAVED
SLIGHTLY SILENT, NOT IN SCREAMS
SOULFULL SOMETHING LIKE THE STREAMS

SINGING SONGSTRESS SING MY SONG
SING IT STANDING TALL AND STRONG
SING IT SOOTHING, SO IT SEEMS
STRONG AND STRIVING THROUGH MY DREAMS!

KILL THE POETS II

Kill the poets

My friend, my love

Kill the poets like God above

Hang them on your walls

Tack them to the board

Kick them in the balls

Where their pain is stored

Kill the poets

Make them all dead

Kill the poets

By putting love in their beds

CHAPTER 2

BRAIN
FARTS!

-THE GRAND SEARCH-

…What am I looking for?
I don't know.
What do I want?
Just to know what I'm looking for…

I think that what I really want is just the knowledge—not the knowledge that enables you to properly converse over intellectual subjects-(whatever that means)-
But the knowledge of life—what is it truly for? A test? A beginning? A blessing or a curse?
The knowledge that one must experience everything in order to want nothing at all. The ability to bring light into the very center of the darkest shadow to see what lurks in it's inky depths—Like the depths of man that can only be seen if you look far enough out.
I want the knowledge to know-
Why that girl laughs-
Why tears fall faster than dreams-
Why love only glances at some and then with others, entangles itself in a life long stare down competition that makes even the by standers eyes water.
I want to know why L. Ron Hubbard can start a religion with what he wrote (tax breaks and all) and I can't even convince the deaf dumb and blind of money filled hands Florida to stop jabbering about their late night excursions and lazy frolics in smoke filled drunken darkness at clubs where the music is too loud to talk, not to mention listen! Maybe it's because I'm not trying to sell a philosophy on life, just an experience of it.

See here I am, venting at my lined paper with violent blows of a pen that bruises it with internal bloody marks that will only heal when fresh eyes water it with their inquisitive caress.

I want this knowledge without even having the knowledge of how to gain it—
I can't even find a job not to mention the key to a knowledge that I don't even
know exists anymore.

I just know, or I think I know that everyone—the strange lonely man with the
face aged by wind and sun in maroon shorts that wanders through towns in
this area—the Mercedes Benz driver who won't get off the cell phone—the
stoned teenagers at the waters edge wondering if they can still swim—the
Grandmother, just here visiting her daughter (or vice versa)—and the daugh-
ter who sits and forces out smiles in dull conversation-
They're all looking, looking around, looking up and down and waiting and
looking—they have been their whole lives—and they may very well for the
remainder—just look-
But for what?
I don't know-
I don't know knowledge-
But does the knowledge know me?

KEEP (Feet in thinking)

I remember thinking about everything all the time walking around with my
hands in my pockets and my eyes on the ground
The future has no excuse for not being here
I've worn myself thin two or three or maybe four times in the past day and I
still blink in amazement at my repetitious feet
Sometimes everything will seem to disappear in the red rivers of my white see-
ing worlds
I turn out the lights for the shortest time possible
Like two suns
Around the same dream

I'm paying the price for past mistakes with change for tomorrow

I hide myself in the dungeon for an escape from the chains my own ideas
clamp around my ankles
Screams come out of the woodwork and neighbors problems
I told myself I would never pay attention—but this time I think she's in the
right
I throw my pillow over my head and my feet into my bed
Sometimes I think my heart will never stop beating
It's like an engine that has grown used to not having an oil change
And I think if I change anything now it will sputter and jerk and all of my
waves of emotion and thought will be thrown through my windshield and
onto the hood of my only protection

I sleep during the day because I don't go there until morning
My nights are filled with laughs and funny friends who look better in that light
I am discreet when I get beat by unsure actions—movements and shadows
that don't move the way anyone wants them to
Maybe I should just sit back and wait
But waiting is something I can not do—not here -not now
I'm running out of change

And so I charge like the devil with red hair
I'm hiding under the bridge searching for your carriage and the perfect opportunity to burn you out of it
But it may have already passed just like this crazy plan

I can see that everything around me is nothing at all unless I can see the true meaning to me
And you dreaming of me—late night—thoughts in the stars reflected in your eyes—and that face in your pupils is so recognizable

I tore apart my insides in hopes the outside would change but now the inside just wants more and I am again the same—the same as yesterday and today—no different to you or me—like a mirror reflection that refuses to leave with the image it portrays
But I'm here—mid day—mid wife—it's time for my bath—wash off this smile for ten cents and a kiss and leave me here to soak up all the people and places and things I've seen and done and thought in these past two seconds

So full of shit it clogs my drain and I get beat again

"You won't know unless you try—You can't laugh unless you cry!" Immortal words from the immortal mother who gave birth to this daily dreamer and thinker because it makes everything so much better when you're here

And the light passes through the window blinds and flashes into my eyes and all I can see is you, standing there smiling like the Joker from Batman—you've just pulled another prank
And just like the Christians on the crusades, taught the Muslims how to kill—I'll teach you how to drown yourself in useless matters so that you too can hide with me in solitude. I don't want to be alone anymore! I'll build myself a cellmate, for or against your will; it really doesn't matter to me—I never told you what I did to my dog!

Sir Tinnley Reel

Certain situations always seem to rush over me like a wave and fill the five gal-lon bucket I constantly keep strapped to my back—(I used to know a man who let problems run off his back like water, but he's gone now—off to be a teen aged girls wet dream) while my bucket weighs me down. My feet move slower and not quite as repetitively
The beat has changed but the song and the girl and the friends and the nights and the smiles are still the same

Do you have a corkscrew I could borrow—just something to pierce the bot-tom of this bucket and open the champagne

I've been here for twenty-two years watching the days fly by as the birds go south and the sun comes up and goes down and the moon will always follow just like my left foot to my right
And I used to talk to her I used to think about her all the time—my dear sweet mother who did everything she could to be my father—she even learned how to hit!
She was golden glove on my childhood street
That beautiful lady—now just a voice over mans brightest but most visually restricting invention

Push the buttons to get through just like you used to do to me

I've seen the good and the bad and I like them both equally—I always try to be fair
But something wont let me talk to you the way I did before
I'll sit on my bedroom floor and imagine all the great things I could say—maybe you'll even understand—but then the sun comes up and it's time to get to bed—I'll keep those ideas in my head—because it's so much better when you're not there

I used to think that in order to dream you had to have a reason—something big and powerful like the ocean—but the glass of water by my head can do the same if not more—it knocks on my door to tell me your secrets

Hidden deep—I see your feet—you're following me—walking along side by side like walls in the hallway
I look over I see myself and you hand me a corkscrew—friends are there no matter how full your bucket
Open the champagne and call my mom just like the dreams
And that is when I realize—the smiles and the laughs—they come wrapped up in people like presents—open them up and it's Christmas day

A box full of reasons and change I can use to pay for past mistakes

Everything is good even when it's bad—that coffee at three A.M.—you bought it to show me another reflection—always something new when I'm with all of you that is why it is so much better when you're here

So I sit and watch some more to see what else there is to say—not much really it's all been said before anyway

I hope you come to see me in a dream land—that's the best time for you to see what I truly think about you—the serum you gave me that makes me speak and tell you this—it works terribly well as you can tell—I take it a lot—this new kind of nectar—straight from the dreams—drained from the brain and into my glass

Drink it up—shhhh! Don't make a sound—I'm thinking about you

I see you and you see me—reflections of each other in red river eyes—tired and drowsy—I'll kiss you good night today because I'm going to be so much better now that you're here

My feet are walking I'm coming to find you—so just stay where you are
I have gifts in return for what you've given me I hope you enjoy them-

A five gallon bucket with a hole in the bottom—an empty bottle of champagne and some spare change for you to keep

WANTED NEEDS OF A DREAMER
OR
(Wanton needs of a screamer)

To want and to need are two terms often confused;
To want is to dream of having; to need is to require.
To want and not be able to receive is pain!
This is the pain I feel. It's not physical; it's not pre-suicidal,
It's just soft, antagonistic pain.

I want love to be a three letter word.
I want pornography to be completely physical.
I want a pair of soft white creamy thigh earmuffs with lunch to boot!
I want to be able to get drunk, act like myself and still get laid!
I want someone to be willing to say to me honestly, that I will see her when I
wake up in the morning, or that she will call me back.
I want cute smiles that turn into grimaces of passionate pain.
I want sex to be hard and sweaty, I want it to make my hair curl.
Then turn to soft caresses of sweet knuckles across my cheek.
I want candy that tastes like a woman!
I want whispers of sweet nothings screamed from passing cars!
I want to play "Where's Waldo?" with someone naked.
I want honest conversation, with undertones of love, (the three-letter word.)
I want headlights and round curves beneath rambunctious sheets.
I want to go toe to toe with my passions.
I want to feel the tensing of every muscle and then the sweet release of every
tense thought and feeling shooting out of my plug and into my friendly little
wall socket!
I want daydreams at night.
I want that anxious moment of the first conversation to last forever.
I want pillow talk that means something.
I want a human hot pad.
I want eyes that see past me and see myself.

Kill The Poets

I want naked hair in my face.

I want hands in my pants that aren't mine!

I want to walk past a store window and see two people instead of just me.

I want massages just because she wants to.

I want silent smiles passing in the street.

I want lips that tease,

A voice that feeds my wants and builds them into uncontrollable desires, two words from being needs.

So close to necessity I am almost needed!

I want time to tell my story.

I want ears that will hear it.

I want to have someone around so that being alone is that much more important!

I want a friend who doesn't preach.

I want to show my mind and be appreciated.

I want to feel the ability to please.

I want to make the world smile and then give a little back.

I want to be on top of the statue that is on my imaginary pedestal!

I want enough money to go anywhere, anytime and bring my mother presents!

I want to know that if I were never at a certain point at a certain time everything would be different!

I want to know why.

I want to know almost everything so that I can know enough but still learn about everything else!

I want to know when I will die so that I can do everything today!

I want soft kisses when things get rough.

I want my love to be known, felt and enjoyed but not taken advantage of.

I want trust and to be trusted.

I want life to be confusing and ridiculous so we can laugh all the time!

I want everyone to know!

I want change.

I want cultural variation in harmony.

I want eyes to turn green with envy and then back to their original color with the satisfaction of knowing I will share!
I want two-foot nipple stages to dance my tongue on!
I want fancy food and candlesticks.
I want manicured eyebrows.
I want long fingers and necks that smell of wanton desires.
I want visual excitement to enhance the colors in this world.
I want freedom, freedom to kiss a stranger only because I want to.
I want fabulous copulation in conversation.
I want attentive eyes and responding ideas.
I want to be heard!
I want to be thought of as myself and not as "one of those guys!"
I want women to admit they love sex as much as I do!
I want to be able to love without being worried about disease.
I want not to be needed.
I need food, water, clothing and shelter.
I dream of so much more!
I know it's out there I just have to find it.
Somewhere in the luxurious lap of an over friendly friend
Or a prostitute that will, without second thought, take a months worth of my pay.

Short Dreams

Yesterday I had a dream, but it was more than just a dream. Too real in my mind to only exists there. The thoughts became physical and manifested into a reality—Not the reality that everyone knows, just the reality of the room inside my head where dreams spend their time to entertain me with subtle suggestions and unique movements only possible in that secret little world.

Sometimes I wonder which world I prefer. The reality of my mind or the reality of the external world? Both excite and amuse; but one I control and escape to nightly.

To escape?

What do I escape from?

A reality I do not and can not control? A reality that has its way with me. Pushes me and pulls me into decisions I, at times, don't want to make? Or do I not escape, but relieve myself of the follies of my life for a spell; always knowing I will return to them within hours.

How ever it is done subconsciously in my mind; the fact of the matter is, I had a dream yesterday that will not remove itself from the huge internal movie screen behind my eyes!

The dream, on the surface, was quite simplistic. I stood in a meadow golden with the weeds and a cautious setting sun. Throughout this vast opening, various trees interrupted the carefully sculpted horizon. One of which I laid beneath, bathing in its shade and enjoying the blanket of the cool breeze. The kind that kisses your exposed skin softly like a woman saying goodbye or a lover before drifting to sleep.

My eyes scanned the scene sporadically with the excitement of a child at an amusement park. While my body lay still in a relaxed state only achieved in complete calm or under the influence of the finer depressants.

The golden cyclorama reminded me of a past love. The love that now only softly exists in the occasional memories of our last kiss.

She was a beautiful girl, from what I remember. Now I have forgotten her eyes and a touch before that loss I had forgotten her hair and just before, her smile. Now the memory is one of only vague shapes in a shadow that accepts no light to illuminate what I believe I once had!

The death of clarity comes slowly but with precise strokes of its fading paintbrush!

I wish I could clean these images from the past but unfortunately they are much too old and fragile to even be touched. I fear that if I even try to reinforce them with a picture or a note that I have tucked away, I will unintentionally void and shatter what is left and finally remember nothing. That I can not live threw. Not now, while these fond memories of my beautiful, as foggy as they are, are all I have to keep my mind with something, anything in the solitude my being now lives!

I saw the sea today. In all of its glory, it hugged the East Coast like an over protective mother. The sea has always amazed me. The way it reflects what surrounds it. You can see images slightly misshapen in its calm waves. Probably the way things really appear we're just too focused on our own little worlds to see beyond them and into the grand view of the nature that surrounds us.

Yet, the sea is accustomed to reflecting what is above it and today, it is not calm. As I stand here and stare down from the boardwalk into its depths, the sea is tormented. It tragically attacks the shore, stripping it of its size and girth. Am I tormented also on this day? I must be because I can't think clearly and I am smoking far too many cigarettes that slowly strip me of my size and girth! Each taking me one step closer with every puff to the inevitable.

I often wonder what will come of me while I sleep. All these dreams that crash in on me; they show me images of the sort no man should know! These dreams are like secret, endless interpretations; but what do they interpret? The past? The present? The future?

If it is the past, what did I miss? I have few memories like what I see in dreams. Is their idea of what has happened to me that much different than my own?

If it is the present, who sneaks in my room at night to whisper these silly antidotes and experiences into my sleeping mind?

If it is the future, what could I have to look forward to but a de-ja-vu on a rainy or lonely day?

You know scientist say that a person can dream the same dream thirty or forty times a night!

If one were to die in sleep would you become trapped in an endless loop of the same dream? Or is one able to add a little bit to each loop? A word, a moment, a gesture, a position, a blink or a smile… And by doing so, eventually change the dream to become what you have always wanted?

Much like the Hindus idea of life; with each life you add something and by doing so; constantly work your way closer to what they call Nirvana.

Dreams and life, life and dreams! The analysis is endless, the idea limitless, the time, much too short!

To Elena
(Shop for what's in stores)

My dear E,

    Do you know that one day—even today, you are going to be better
Than the scene and the me that you just sat across from. Traveling your
Travels so that you may travel south of the equator. Poaching poachers
And beating on a drum telephone to your favorite neighbor thirty miles away,
Just to spread rumors about the bitch who lives across the rain forest like
Some kind of beat driven gossip fence!

    Just do one thing for me
Just one thing will make me happy and complete-
Don't save your days!
Like 5 to 9 desk schmoozing, BMW driving sick little monkeys!
Don't save them for your vacation time-
Don't save them for personal days-
Don't save them for a bad hangover-
Don't save them for anyone or anything-
What people don't realize is there is <u>no</u> holding place for days.
Days go away as fast as they came to stay!
You can't keep them once they die!
So spend—spend—spend!!

Spend them on knowledge and learning-
Spend them on shoes and friends-
Dirty streets and silly little happenings
That don't really mean a thing once that day is spent!
Find your eyes seeing everything from
Gold watch windows etched with some money made mystery
To little kids walking streets with no food or shoes on their feet-
Find your eyes in bistros and truck stops-
Find them in drunken stupors and libraries-

Find them over looking the sun set in the mountains
And then being forced shut by the pain of salt—water spray!

Don't waste, save, neglect or regret a single day-
Spend them all and spend them wisely-
Only then will you be as wise as you will be!

Remember this and rue the day you forget-

The day you die is the day
You'll know all you'll ever know-
Will your glass be half empty
Or half full?

Choices are made
Plans are forgotten
See the future
And what it's got in
Store!

As Always, Uncle—

SUDS OF BEER

When the weight of night
And the pressure of everyday
Flank your mind-
Like two fingers to a zit
Spueing memories all over
The reflection of your present self
And creating the locations
Of future blemishes-

That's when you know life is too short
To try to wash memories away
With the hot water of time
Or the suds of beer!
Everything has a reason
And every clogged pore comes to a point!

-DID YOU KNOW
WE ARE WHORES-

Do you know what makes your blood move?
Does your soft sensitive skin
Recall the fleeting pleasure of a simple caress?

DID YOU KNOW WE ARE WHORES?

Late night—early morning in a dark room
The words spin like minarets
Hanging in a breeze-
The brazen texture of speech
Without passion or thought
Burns in ears and minds-
The sea of questions can't even douse the fire!

We are lead to believe
By people who do not-
If you don't open the book you'll never know how it ends!
Lemmings do cannon balls
To impress those who follow-
Individuals are alone in the meat market-
Standing in the corner
bearing witness to the slaughter of free minds-
Staring blankly into space wondering
What's between the stars!

Girls and boys are playing games
In bar rooms and on street corners
Just east of lust-
And if you don't play the game how can you ever win?

DID YOU KNOW WE ARE WHORES?

Silent vigils in malls and on beaches-
The sand is the mind of the Earth
The sea, society-
Constantly taking and giving-
We see ourselves through all other eyes
And through that sight we slowly go blind!

Adhere! Adhere! Heed the warnings!
If you don't do as others do
No one will respect you except you-
Except you—accept you!

More nights in dreamy memories of comfortable vigor
With girls I knew before-
Always wondering who will be the next to wake up and say-
Hey, wanna do it again?
The pain of too much-
Poor buddy, red and irritated
He won't speak to me for days-
But at least when he does
He'll mean what he says!

False words and fake actions
Only amount to a vaguely remembered night
That may have never happened-
Words that mean to insight a dream
Or kick the mind to think-
Coupled with a touch warm enough to turn your heart back to red-
Will make memories that you set on repeat!

Fuck my mind, then fuck me!
Teach me you, then we'll screw!

All these people who walk with their
Trophies dragging behind them-
They never smile-
Some people don't get the point-
You can accomplish more with one thing that is real
Than you can with a thousand fading nights
Of pick-up lines
And sex that probably wasn't that good any way!

DID YOU KNOW WE ARE WHORES?

When will we wake up and smell
The rose colored virus?
When will we open our eyes
And show our true beauty to the world?
When will the lemmings stop?
When will we take our needs for granted?

Bodies and skin and bruises
And sweat and cum and vaginal mucus
And swirling sounds-
Like carnivals falling-
Collide in one room!
Smacking and banging against each other
Like pissed off relaxation balls!

But the souls mesh-
Sweet and subtle
In complete silence-
Only your shadow knows it's happening…

DID YOU KNOW WE ARE WHORES!

-PROTEUS-

The many disguises
Of the many days
People change with every situation
Every breeze can move
A mood to a different scene

When we laugh
We do because others do
When we cry
We do because others do
When we hide
It is because others run us off
When we expose all
It is because others make us feel comfortable
And able to open locked doors

Proteus lives within us all-
Changing and changing and changing
To escape the enemies of self-consciousness
We are all the same
Just constantly changing our shapes
At different times to stay individual

Oh, the complexities of our human kind!

OPTIMISTIC SHOES

optimism gets lost in unspoken ideas like love that isn't chased

i could have done it—I could have been there and made the right move at the right time…
but I was too content with the simplistic caress and my fingers slipped and I dropped my cup full of opportunity.
It shattered on my floor and ran away like an unwanted pet.

who has ever done everything right?
-like a one armed man-
who knows themselves well enough to control their fate?
to know when and where to move in this trivial chess game?
-my king is too short to see over the pawns-

I walked once, everywhere I ever wanted to go—but the sky was green and the clouds wouldn't rain, the sun shone through everything I believed was real, so now I am unsure as to what is true and false and in between in this little world, I have to relearn everything!
-someone erased my chalk board and left me hanging-

we all have fears and worries and that is natural for this frightening world, like grass and trees and disease.
But some of us dwell too long on the wrong worries.

I always close my mouth like a time locked safe; it only opens when I'm alone.
-optimism, don't hide in a half empty idea-

I can't look you in the eyes and tell you what I see and think and feel.
I want it again, that feeling, that uncontrollable tidal wave of chill through my body from just five simple fingertips.
Amazing drug, that feeling of being someone's comfort, someone's very own pillow or security blanket.

-optimism, the human minds way of feeling good no matter what monster is eating you from the inside out-

if I believed everything I ever said I think I would have grown another nose for my new face.
-so sarcastic, so unbelievable-

my optimism that every thing will always go wrong or fall through like a dry rotted floor trying to hold a grand piano.
-music by means of gravity-

am I reactionary because I want to go back to the hay day when my horse had enough food?
Am I a radical because I want something new?
Do you?

I love the feeling but the situation terrifies me, like a b-film actress with a man-eating dung beetle nipping at her ankles!
-optimism tells me it's fake-
but then again so could everything I say
-optimism-

so much comfort, so much sensation that disappeared as fast as it showed up.
-optimism, so worried if it's real-

fear and security and smiles and tears all mixed into one, like Irish coffee, my brain doesn't know which way to run!
Up and down and all around I'm dizzy!

People touch but do they feel?
We try to live in reality but do we realize?

Everything is so different in everyone else's mind. My picture is painted with black and white finger paints and everyone else seems to be oil and water based colors with crocodile hairbrush strokes.

I could speak and tell you all what I feel is truth but that could be fact tomorrow and as we all know fact is as far from the truth as everything I just said.
-optimism?-

can things change like a haircut or leaves in the fall?
Or will I always question myself and everything I do?
Question it until it becomes so ridiculous that even to do it I would have to wear a mask and disguise my voice like Jack Nicholson or a talking dog.
My hands shake and spill my Irish coffee whenever I think of risking anything that has to do with my emotions.
Am I conservative because of this?
Will I be stigmatized as Newt Gingrich because I have canceled the art of feelings in fear they may one-day control?
-optimism-

hidden away like Atlantis are all my ideas and thoughts that I talked myself into and out of in a split second...
-the quick thinker that I am-
like a computer that only finds problems, it doesn't solve them.

Am I walking backwards or am I just looking in the wrong direction?

Good things happen but good dreams never turn out the way I saw them on my built in movie screen.
-I'm idealistic not optimistic-
ideal optimism, impossible-

I look up and see the brilliant stars just like the eyes next to me and I feel the warm sun and cool breeze just as easily as the next self-contained thought factory.
-does anyone process ideas like I do?-

they seem so good when they first pop up but after many hours of careful editing and the moment of truth when they are to be executed I pull the switch and burn them in fear of anything I can think of to be afraid of.

How would people react if they found out I did this crazy thing and got dissed like an empty soup can?
-optimism makes me think too much-

I light a cigarette and look at the hot, like a volcano, I have control of a volcano! My mind is a volcano! It's red and shinny and black and dull and half-burned out by dead thoughts that haven't been flicked away yet. It could blow away, and then I could see what it melted into. A mold of myself to investigate!
-Columbo optimism-

if I could tell you all right now, that everything every one of you has ever given me individually, I have saved in a very special place in my mind. Every hug and kiss and word and look and quick winks and hand shake and conversation and smile and worry and question, its all put away in here for future smiles when you're not around.
Tucked back in a manila folder labeled, "for a solitary day."
Is that optimism?
Or could that be considered remembering the past because the future is too unknown?
-optimism?-

I know I am safe here but there was that one five minute movie that actually happened to me, it turned me in so many directions at the same time I thought I might be a discombobulated blob of insecure open hearted optimism!

Think good and if it falls short you feel like a minaret.
Think bad and if it falls bad you're still the same shoe size.
Am I wrong for wanting to still fit in my clothes?

NATURES REST

Did you know that the ants and the honeybees will always love their Mothers?

Even as the street trolleys grow complacent in their worn ruts in downtown, where the buildings rise up like dandelions or shrines to yet another artificial God, this one called "Something Inc.,"

Where trees grow with their roots constricted by concrete and stones! Their branches, light by the lack of birds' nests, reach and reach for the sky! Attaining nothing but smog.

Down town, where the mountains in the distance rage and blow clouds over the city to ensure that we never forget they will always be more majestic!

The clouds look down and smile at the people running against clocks that they invented and will never stop! Not ever realizing that they can!

Where cars drive by burning old buried bones and "Toot!" their virtueless horns!

In this place there is no nature, there is no rest!

Just the nature of man and the rest of us!

AND THE CLOWN GOES DOWN

AREYOUHAPPYTODAYMYDEARCOLOREDCLOWNYOUKNOWYOUCAN
NEVERBEIFSMILINGWITHSOMEONEELSESTEETHANDWEARINGA
PAPERCROWNSWIMMINGTHROUGHTHOUGHTSYOUTRIEDSO
DESPERATLYTODROWNHOWWETDOYOUFEELNOW?
STAREATTHEBUBBLESTHATRACEYOUTOTHESURFACEAND
WITHTHEMTAKETHECOLORINYOURSKINSOMEONEFORGOT
THEIRPURPOSESOMEONEFORGOTHOWTOSWIM!
YOURMAKE-UPISRUNNINGAWAYWITHYOURSMILEASYOUFLAIL
ANDSCREAMNOWYOU'REDYINGWITHSTYLE!
WHOWILLDRINKYOURGRAVE-AREYOUPARCHEDENOUGH?
CANYOUHEARTHEREQUIEMMARCHINMAY?
KICKTHEDEPTHSWITHALLYOURMIGHTIFYOUTRYHARDENOUGH
THEYJUSTMIGHTRELEASESOMELIGHT!
SOTIREDNOWSOTIREDTIREDOFWEARINGTHEOILPAINTSOF
ANOTHER-GOCHOIRGOCHOIRPLEASESINGMESOMETHING
OTHERTHANPOISIDENSLASTATTIRE!
IT'SSODARKNOWALLTHETHINGSTHATMADEYOUNOTYOUARE
GONESOMEHOWANDYOUARELEFTINTHEDARKEMPTYNOTHING
WEREYOUEVERSOMETHING?
GOODBYEMYCLOWNIKNOWWE'LLSEEYOUAGAINAROUNDTOWN
THENEXTTIMEIDECIDETODRINKYOUDOWN
DISAPPEARINGWITHONELASTBUBBLEANDABURPTHATBRINGS
UPYOURCOLORFULCROWN.

CHAPTER 3

THE PARTY GEAR
THE BEER
AND
THE GAS

THE PARTY GEAR THE BEER & THE GAS

Nine a.m. on Friday morn,
The party was to be tonight.
But, I have to tell you, I was sore
And moving this early wasn't quite right.

The phone was screeching,
Screaming in my head!
I answered with annoyance
From the edge of my bed,

"What the hell do you want?!" I said,

The voice on the other end
Was none other than my faithful girlfriend—

"Jesus Christ, you ass! Sometimes you're so sass!
Now get off your ass! It's time to get the party gear
The beer and the gas."

Slumping a little,
Not wanting to go,
I then responded
A quite bit slow,

"All right lady,
I'll be there soon,
But if I'm getting up now
We're starting drinking at noon!"

"Alright, hurry up!"
She said, as she always does.
Clicking the phone line, from voices,

To nothing but fuzz.

I raised myself in my bed
And let a fart loft.
After some moments of contemplation,
Picking my nose and minor coughs
I got in the shower
To wash the sleep off.

Then I went to brew coffee,
As if on a mission!
I slid on the linoleum
Into my kitchen.
There, I ran into Duey,
Whose face was always twitch'n!

"Hey Duey, what's going on?"
I said as I turned the pot on.
"Nothing but my hangover
And last night's biggest con."

He mumbled, thumbing over his shoulder
As a young lady, eighteen, no older
Slowly entered my sight
Like a lost puppy or the moon on a cloudy night.

"Good morning miss," I said,
As I blew her a kiss.
She just turned red
As Duey's face twitched.

"I'm off to the store!"
I yelled, as they passed,
"To pick up the party gear,

Sir Tinnley Reel

The beer and the gas!"

"O.K." said Duey,
In a solemn voice.
Obviously the girl
Was a drunken Duey choice.

As I walked out
I asked Duey to straighten the house,
He said he would
As soon as he got off the couch.

And so I left,
Knowing full well
He wasn't getting off that couch,
Neither was his smell!

Duey and the girl
Sat there in silence.
When he had nothing to say,
Duey was always quiet.

Enter from the basement
A Jovial Jew
Smelling of a weed scent
And morning dew!

"Hey kid!"
He said to Duey, with some spit.
"Tonight's the party,
I'll need another lid!"

"After you clean up
I'll call the connection man
Duey responded
Without even trying to stand.

The Jew retorted,
"Duey you don't understand!
I just smoked my last bowl
And that was all the resin I had!"

"Then you'd better clean,
I'll call the weed man when I choose!"
The situation understood,
"Alright, some cleaning I'll do!"

As I returned with Lavern,
And everything we had,
The party gear, the beer
And the gas;

I saw Duey, just as he was,
The quiet girl moved just for fun,
But the house was clean,
Perfectly done!

Then I spotted Jew, smiling,
"I see you got the stuff,"
He said, as he rolled a big one,
"You want a puff?"

"No, no, not right now."
I replied, walking to the kitchen,
"I've too much to do
In order to make this party bitch'n!"

Sir Tinnley Reel

"Bitch'n, Huh?"
He said, with a pull.
Handed it to Lavern
And beat on his skull.

"What time does it start?"
He yelled through the door.
As Lavern hit the joint, I said,
"Oh, three or four."

Then I was accosted
By Lavern with a kiss
Coupled with her last breath
And fine Marijuana mist!

I inhaled the second hand smoke
And it was grand!
I returned her the kiss
And quickly shook Jew's hand.

"Oood stuff!"
I said, not wanting to release.
"Yeah, but to get the best buzz
You really should breathe."

Said the Jew with a smile,
The joint between his teeth.

Duey turned to us,
With face flushed he said,
"I think after tonight
I'll either be retarded or dead!"

The silent girl laughed,
A surprise to us all!
Lavern quickly asked,
"What are you called?"

The girl, still a lot shy,
Used an amusing, almost silent reply.
With nothing but her feet
In her concentrating eyes,

"People call me Ashton,
But you can call me Dread,
It's the name Duey gave me
Last night in his bed."

We all, unsurely nodded
And told her our names,
Duey just sat there
Not saying a thing.

Then, the clock struck noon!
And finally it was time to...
TO LAY THE PREMISE
FOR THE COMING AFTERNOON!!

I looked to Lavern
And she looked to the Jew
Who looked over at Duey
And the little Dread girl too!

"Alright people,
The time is so true!

Sir Tinnley Reel

Accept your responsibilities,
You know what to do!"

Immediately everyone in the room
Began to move...

Lavern ran to the kitchen
And grabbed five brews,
As I threw the zigzags
To the Jovial Jew,
Who was priming the tank
And filling the balloons!

Dread ran to the shower
And Duey did too!
"We're having people over," I yelled,
"So clean up the goo!"

We set up the house
As fast as we could!
We set out the food
And chilled the beer as we should!
We filled it with balloons
And colorful banners,
The house was done up
In a grandiose manner!

As we completed our
Preparing tasks
The party gear, the beer and the gas
Duey and Dread re-entered at last.

"Perfect timing, you clean little fools!"
Shouted the not so Jovial Jew,
"Everything was done
While you worked your tool!"

Duey, just twitching and sipping his beer said,
"Sorry, but I have to go easy on Dread,
She's just a little bum,
Not so experienced in the shower as some."

Dread was behind him frozen in fear,
Then, like a bullet that just missed your ear,
She shouted in a whisper
But her message was clear!

"They don't have to know that
You freaky little man!
What we do alone
Is no business for them!"

Dread was so mad
She had white-knuckle fists!
Lavern hurried over
To help resolve this.

"Duey, I swear sometimes
You can be so queer!"
Duey just smiled,
Twitched and drank his beer.

Then Jew jumped in
With a statement in jest,
"Well, voyeurism isn't quite sex
But it's exciting none the less!"

Sir Tinnley Reel

Everyone giggled and
Laughed a little bit.
Even pissed off Dread,
Now over her fit.

"When's everyone gonna be here?"
Lavern asked, grabbing another beer.
"Hopefully soon." I said,
"Hey, grab me one dear!"

The clock lumbered by,
But soon it was time
As some of the guests
Began to arrive.

The first to show
Were Cubberlabe and Go,
Already drinking
As they passed the window.

Go swung the door open
Cubberlabe right behind,
"Hey, where's the fucking party?
We were expecting a line!"

"Ahh, sit down and shut up you freaks
From the city of hippies and stone!"
I said, with a belittling tone.
"Watch your mouth Fried
Or I'll show you a stone,
Right here in my fist!
I'll crack you in the nose
And then in the lips!"

Kill The Poets

"Hey, hey, hey fellas!"
Interrupted the Jew.
No need to fight!
We've got better things to do!

He whipped out a bowl and said,
"Speaking of stones,
Why don't you help me with this?
I hate smoking alone!"

So we all circled the table
And cashed that bowl out!
Getting all of us pretty looped
Without a doubt.

Then walked in
The Man From Another Planet
Or MFP:
The name he demanded.

Eyes glassed over
And a smile on his face.
A piano over his shoulder,
Where ever he goes, he plays!

"MFP!"
We all shouted with glee!
As he walked across the room
Wasted as can be.

"I started a little early,
I hope you don't mind?
You know how it goes
When one finds some free time."

Sir Tinnley Reel

"Grab yourself a beer,
Take off your piano and stay."
Duey said with authority,
In his usual way.

Soon the house began to fill
With Jerry's, Geoff's
Jenny's and Jill's!
Everyone was there
With brain cells to kill!
Even some we didn't know,
Having drinks and popping pills!

The debauchery increased
As the night moved towards its peak.
Drinking, smoking
And some people speaking Greek!

The party got louder
As more began to meet.
The beer flowed like water,
The balloons never ceased!

Smoke filled every room,
It almost hurt to breathe.
But no one would stop
Until their minds began to bleed!

Somewhere in the background
A band began to scream!
Playing magical sounds,
Making the non-sleeping dream!

Kill The Poets

MFP beat on the ebonies
With malicious speed,
Go thumped the Bass,
Jew, on guitar, smoking more weed!

The party got so big
We thought it might crash
Until Duey and Dread appeared
With more of the party gear, the beer and the gas!

The circus picked up,
As inhibitions fell down!
There were Falacios and Fornicators
Tinkering all around!

This event spun like a centrifuge
Way out of control!
There was no escape
From the panty patrol!

Girls were teasing
With their eyes and their hands.
The boys were laughing
And doing the horny dance.

We were headed in a direction
No one had ever planned!
Love and laughter, boys and girls,
Hand in hand!

Duey ran up to me
In the midst of a scream,
"I've had a psychic vision,
A weird kind of dream!

All of these people are gonna fuck tonight
In our living room of green!"

Then he suddenly ran away,
With his hands throwing whipped cream,
His gapping mouth
Still stuck in that scream!

Eventually,
Even this party wound down.
"Too many relaxants,
I'm too close to the ground!"
Jew said slow,
With almost no sound.

I observed the party
And was happy to see
All these people so open heartedly
Slipping into their fantasies!

I couldn't believe our house
So full, so fast!
Of people enjoying
The party gear, the beer and the gas!

Shortly you could see
The pairs in the scene.
People gravitating to each other,
Like grass and autumn leaves.

Duey and Dread had now disappeared.
Someone said screams could be heard
Coming from Dueys room in the back hall.
Turns out Dread wasn't that inexperienced at all!

Kill The Poets

Every stranger in the house
Seemed to have found a friend
All I saw in the living room
Were naked tits and rear ends!

Jew was in a kitchen chair
With a chic on his lap.
I walked over there
And gave him a tap,

"Well, my friend
If it's voyeurism you want,
It's in the living room
With the sexual savants!"

The next thing I knew,
He and his friend
Disappeared into the sea
Of curves and bends!

"This party is amazing!
Not a lonely soul in sight!"
I said to Lavern
Who was beginning to bite!

"The sun blinds you through the day
Of all the secrets hidden after twilight!"
She replied as she grabbed
My hand and squeezed it tight!
Then yanked me towards my room
To call it a night!

As we walked through
The living room again,

Sir Tinnley Reel

I couldn't help peaking to spy
The positions they were in!
Picking up some tips
For my own night of sin!

We got to my room and closed the door,
Knowing full well we would, once again, wake up sore.

We were abruptly awakened
By the screech of the phone
And Duey screaming out,
"LEAVE US ALONE!"

Lavern and I,
Duey and Dread,
All met Jew in the living room
With pains in our heads.
But the house was amazing!
You should've seen where it went!

It was quite a scene!
Of bare backs and knees!
Everyone was on anyone,
Wrapped up, asleep!

A boob here!
A puss there!
Satisfied lovers
Everywhere!

You wouldn't believe
How we waved with pride,
As everyone, quite sluggishly,
Said their good byes.

Kill The Poets

When the house was empty,
Leaving just the five,
We all sat at the table
Barely alive.

Until we started letting out
Little happy laughs,
As we passed around the last
Of the party gear, the beer and the gas!

copyright 1999 Sir Tinnley Reel

Sir Tinnley Reel

WRITERS BLOCK?

Blank blank blankety blank
Blink blunk blunkety blink
Blinkety blank blank
Blunkety blunk blank blink!

Blankety blink blank
Blinkety blank blink
Blunkety blank blank
Blinkety blank blink!

Blunkety blink
Blunkety blank
Blunkety blank blink
Blankety blink blank!

Blankety blankety blank!
Blunkety blunkety blink!
Blinkety blinkety blank!
I should've had a drink!

0-595-24512-9

Printed in the United States
755400003B